jumping in the asylum

jumping in the asylum

Patrick Friesen

QUATTRO BOOKS

The publication of *jumping in the asylum* has been generously supported by the Canada Council for the Arts and the Ontario Arts Council.

 Canada Council **Conseil des Arts**
for the Arts **du Canada**

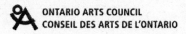 **ONTARIO ARTS COUNCIL**
CONSEIL DES ARTS DE L'ONTARIO

Author's photograph: Marijke Friesen
Cover design: Marijke Friesen
Editor: Allan Briesmaster
Typography: Grey Wolf Typography

Every effort was made to find the owner of the photograph of Nijinsky in the asylum.

Library and Archives Canada Cataloguing in Publication

Friesen, Patrick
    Jumping in the asylum / Patrick Friesen.

Poems.
Issued also in electronic format.
ISBN 978-1-926802-57-2

    I. Title.

PS8561.R496J84 2011   C811'.54   C2011-903992-3

Published by Quattro Books Inc.
89 Pinewood Avenue
Toronto, Ontario, M6C 2V2

Printed in Canada

CONTENTS

He wondered about the word, so filled with breath
yet breathless, breathless, breathless. A full stop.

(P.K. Page from "Cullen in the Afterlife")

crows

those fucking crows those four brilliant gawking crows
    almost shoulder to shoulder on the roof's ridge
that oily sun and the pale cloth of sky slim fingers
    shaping the thin bone of a perfect blue cloud
the crows have wrecked the street with their curses
    they preen in anticipation and are ready

the bushes and trees are silent and reach for a possible
    suicide from the lunging balcony above
and those four crows in their purple soutanes and
    birettas nodding as they wait for someone to emerge
they are patient though they sidle sideways and pause
    sideways and pause finding another view

the work of crows is sometimes the work of murder
    but always the work of witness and last rites
the cloud has charred and begun to crumble falling in
    flakes in soot and ashes all over the world
the crows hunch beneath the ash growing grey and
    annoyed as they endure a death that no one sees

storm windows

wrenching open the shed door squeal and must squashed
    plums underfoot and looking for storms
cans of dry paint a hammer and handsaw hanging from
    nails an old blue bicycle with flat tires
your children in the corner startle you a bird dead at their
    feet they're digging a grave with a trowel

you stand there it's enough standing there unseen and
    becoming snow your weight drifting off
a handclap a sudden thunder and you whirl toward the
    door it's you what did you think it's you
your children are laying the bird to rest their hands are
    calling the rituals only children know

there is a place you will live you know that there is a
    place where you will meet yourself for a moment
what did you think your children gone into the world and
    the bird singing what did you think?
you haul out the windows to clean for the winter you will
    bend your back today what did you think?

daughter

bareheaded with the dark hair of a thousand years of
    fields and infidels the lanterns moon and silhouette
who clothed her in the naked summer who placed her
    in the garden grown from ancient seeds?

barefoot in a pale green dress brown eyes squinting as
    she whirls in surprise to see who calls
on the anvil of july hollyhocks and the dark inside of
    the tin shed the oily grass smell of the mower

stunned for a moment in the back yard slowed by the
    syrup of humid air and sun and the rasp of bees
she bends at the waist and moves to begin her gaze
    away and her long arms spread exquisite

she tilts between beck and flow sowing a voice and
    everything turns and turns again and everything goes on
juice drooling from fallen plums bark peeling from the
    birch and the sky blanched as apocalypse

who calls her among the tools the rakes and hoes who
    calls her through her feet to her hair?
who calls calling a slender stream a fish of rivers and
    rushes calling from the dark arch of the bridge?

still life without einstein

can't do it can't hold an apple in the light can't look at it
    long enough to become no time at all
or limes in the spanish bowl green thunder rolling low
    through quaking aspen and balsam poplar

can't think that green not the green that moves and won't
    be still the green that green doesn't know
carve your thumbnail into orange peel and the scent
    overwhelms colour and abandons shape

can't hold up the sky there is no structure for that but the
    blue curve that comes to light as thought
the arc of the mind's traffic hands and knees toward what
    can't be reached passing what's left behind

and in the window who is that washing the woman's feet
    his face in shade but not his long hands
he leans into light to kiss her feet but einstein has left and
    no one paints still life anymore

pale sky amnesia

hangman's drop and nothing left of bloodline and shaky
  recall can't write any of it that's enough of history
slant light off the page glares in your cataract eyes what
  do you do with that bifurcation of earth and world?
damn the choir and all its lies no one ever told the truth
  among others perhaps no one told a truth

enough of the lights show tune gospel show and *schauen*
  sirrah sirrah looking back at that *augenblick*
boy young man in your dotage in all your agitation old
  man on a back street raw and child in your defeat
give me that blackout fugue the water of the *seine* the
  water water of mother rain give me the long rain

let fall rain the broken bread and alcohol of god let fall daily
  bread prayer the unsayable you must leave for good
not anything but eye sigh and scent what you never in your
  short eternal life wish to name or claim
fading photograph and pale sky amnesia that afternoon
  rapture all of you away in a shudder

it's no messiah none of that play and stage it never ends
  that way it's always always *dénouement*
ah they try the prophets and the mystics they work for
  absolution and nakedness they go eerie
the others dig their spuds and churn the butter but that's
  another life everyone mounts the steps

our leaving and our leaving again

the house of night with the broken wall trying to hold you
    a smudged glass on the end table
whose shoe on the balcony rail the other in the shrubs
    below it is easy to forget where you have gone
saint christopher hanging from a branch and flies
    everywhere this was never the consoling fetish
a glass fell inside but only cracked open the dark sweet
    blood of alcohol spreading on the grey rug
and no one raised their arms for you their arms too
    heavy with the sorrows they had claimed

you are a collector of shoes scuffed shoes or shoes
    without laces your closet is filled with them
each evening you open the sliding doors to take
    measure of the footwear to begin a night of accounting
there is fatigue here the stories are too young for this old
    place fatigue and pleasure in the usual things
you will know the night you wake up with your last pain
    the only pain to matter in your life
sitting on the edge of your bed looking down one foot
    feeling for the slippers just out of reach

between night at the dark window and faint light beneath
    the door a woman is turning on her side
outside you hear the watery sigh of weather the sound
    of birth and the quick arrival of rain
where you are and where you've been the only age is
    earth the only age we have lived and left
there is no mystery but our leaving and our leaving again
    that mystery of strangers at the station
half-awake and glancing at the clock as if all these things
    run on time she smiles and calls for a cab

rousing in a dream of root and slough

some nights you're naked and groan squirming within your
    will or whatever you call that toad
slumbering in your smell and stew rousing in a dream of
    root and slough and a warm sloppy rain

incinerating in a furnace the heat from an old fire a heat
    that doesn't know a damn about romance
nothing galahad nor gawain nothing of ribbons of bows not
    a thing of moon or shield or *death do us part*

it's heat and raw sugar like waking in new orleans sweating
    as if you've copulated all night long
everything happened that could in the fever of sleep arching
    and scorched the blanket thrashed to the floor

in the night shambles of carnival you are naked fuel for the
    yellow tumbling hair of the moon
you have lain with smooth anthea with corinna in may and
    you have loved a woman without a name

bombed by the sun

hawk and body the meat of glory begotten all begotten
    the ragged pine the thistle the ruffed grouse
blueflies at the window the sting of pleasure and bee
    hum look who could know god in the details
who could and did come to words snake and shape lines
    wavering in the sand dirt and wind
how do you remember a moment one july day in 1952
    how do you write it with your arms and eyes?
that sill you stepped across somewhere on home street
    flat-out on the sidewalk bombed by the sun

you almost hear what you saw eating tomato sandwiches
    in someone's life the day of your birthday
it doesn't matter when the juice runs down your chin
    when it ran down your chin and you licked it back
the women singing happy birthday on a blanket and you
    sang something else behind your hand
it's no requiem not this kind of singing your mother's
    clear voice keeping the others in tune
a hangdog dog a face you have to love not yours not
    anymore if ever a face before all the others

that red-winged blackbird at pentecost hovering above
    the marsh and the life of the buried child
your daughter's beads around your wrist and the round
    prayers there reminding you of no road
and you're underground with the dark taste of earth
    words of seed and worm and birth birth birth
black casket rolling down the aisle an old woman in
    her black dress and rose-spattered shawl
no sermons oh christ only the blowfly glittering blue
    and green on her brow only her old old smile

a scar that remains a beauty mark a sin like horses in their
    full smell coming to light from the bush
the faint drone of an old chevrolet dusting down town
    line road carrying the fever of a wanton kiss
a plowman's gull white-bellied against blue sky banking
    south and gliding toward the nuisance ground
grandfather good jesus grandfather smiling through some
    golden window half-blinded with sun
and sun rolling you among the stones as it rolled you
    before as it rolled you from the beginning and more

you can't go back to deny or retrieve you don't deal in
    those lies if you live there is nothing to take back
to have spread your arms at the hotel door to have
    stepped into the next sun or moon to have been a man
not much to rely on but the kid on his fulcrum no hands
    ma look and rolling through the morning mist
sitting for hours beside a pond cosmology on his brain
    and him inside the voluptuous transcendent mess
and the hawk yes it's there drifting through ages of sky
    its gaze and always the little animal

there may be no god in the womb there is a life the fishy
    life of the fetus at the door of the world
thunder shakes the glass rain and hail scour trees and a
    mother moans in the throes of her certainty
it is good this soiled place is it good and holy is this
    where a father stands up hands raised in ambiguity?
and here are we silent knowing nothing but that we make
    bold and go out toward this awful place?
women are singing as the moon rises above your old
    birthday and nighthawks open the dark

the water that remembers

the pink squalid pudge of you the child in its sucking lust
    hands and mouth and beginning to forget
the water that remembers rivers carrying soil and shine
    light flowing over the grinding wheel

the animal dies and often love and sometimes fear runs
    through your nerves but the river only fails
you find the funeral itch and bliss all you might need
    the seed you swallow from an ancient tree

in the heat and years of your summers dazed and brained
    like goya's dog looking up at all that sky
and it's coming down like a foot you learning how to walk
    quick and sideways heaven in the shade

you know barely what tore you apart the knitting that was
    done purl one purl two and the lost stitch
how long do they watch over you? how long the undoing
    at their fingers? these merciless ones

water runs around you a soft obstacle something like the
    gods who spin stories on their looms
sometimes you remember all of that and every once in a
    while you recall what came before

son

you were dancing in some rural wedding hall your daughter
    on your feet her small hands holding on
how do you account for seething pinpoints of worlds in the
    night sky and you moving in a drunken rhythm?

sick with smoke and finding your way to the unlit motel
    you found your way to your lost wife
your son waiting for you beyond the flesh big-eyed smiling
    and turning his face toward you

reaching for a milky sea summoning the sailor from his
    ghost ship where he stood ancient watch
overboard on high seas a swimmer swimming canals and
    straits swimming for a harbour of sun

the boy found then in his muscular rush through reeds and
    fables spun in a circle and breaking in
half-dead in his bulky arrival purple cord around his
    throat and blood coursing through the delta

alexandria seville or winnipeg all flowing rivers of
    passage and light in those narrow streets
accidents of encounter of human wish and ambition blind
    want and sorrow and what's remembered

and the man born a child one of the unchosen blown astray
    by storm squall or blue prairie wind
born a son into mothering and fathering born into his own
    loneliness within the lonely tale

solace

take the pleasure of water or muscatel of the coal
    smoldering beneath your garden take that pleasure
find it scattered and forgotten the only pleasure gone
    like the hummingbird or the buried seed

you may need a city to gather your thoughts a place to
    unsettle enough to find what's been lost
you may need a book to be your city a brothel you've
    dreamed or the sailor's song of land's end

death can be sentimental when it's not abstract do you
    imagine your own or do you imagine all the others?
what is it you want in the graveyard where you wander
    reading the names of your recent dead?

your heart racing with radio news with blight and worry
    with the contagion of greed and fear
take the pleasure of the dead they're true now what you
    remember is what you need and maybe more

you want drunkenness or the night something that takes
    you into the presence of your solitude
take the pleasure of your mouth the measure of song
    and talk the gossip of your sudden life

you're the boy who killed himself once before who let
    his blood flow into the pleasure of the earth
you hesitated on the bank of that river before you
    sheered from the spook of milk and honey

when wind plays with light among the aspen leaves and
    you're befuddled once again by your eyes
there is solace in the guitar and the clapping of hands
    in the ways we come again to darkness

jumping in the asylum

are you ravaged fire licking along your arms?
you have memorized photographs words and hands
what flinches at the corner of your eye are you raptured?
remember nijinsky how he stood in the asylum
black shoes and suit remember how he leapt suddenly up
heels together his shadow haunting the wall behind him

that lift and why? miles of neuron and synapse a chemistry
and remember the ghost of a rose and splendour but why?
in the hall in the miles of hall and walls and the current
pulsing cellular through the young man gone
gone with his secret smile gone into the rooms and halls
into the old man who leaped for himself and the other yes

why and when there is no why are you raptured?
arms flayed are you ravished? milk brother to jeanne
losing all for the voice listening defiant and mute
the old man hanging there his hands fluttering beside him
what wasn't called but spoke from fibre and mash brain-
born and sparking the points a hammer on snarling iron

are you seared in the conflagration are you?
hooved yellow-eyed and slender with hunger
it paces before the window yammering in the dark
nerves of words and the clicking of bones picked clean
throats of birds and early light among the leaves
high in the trees there where it begins are you ravaged?

a child's face and a memory of first obliteration
awe and breaking the lost bride of that shadow
his hands small quick souls on their way to death
do you whistle where you loiter are you raptured?
the current through him through all the grey scaffolding
a torrid nonchalance of rufous pistil and stamen

the hall is empty a cleaner sweeping dust and shade
do you smell perfume in wisps do you know?
a person is not a person in the marathon of sperm and eggs
who is light enough to separate who is chaff?
culled from the bone fire raked and combed to grass
there must be a way to leave the earth behind

dragging the river

combing the bottom of the dark river for a disappearance
    a wrinkle on water and then an absence
the raking of water of the unseen and hauling up the
    detritus of town wheels ropes and rust

dragging the river for the child lost abruptly in the river's
    door and in the heat of a july afternoon
could there be such vast want to be water to rock in that
    light where it bends and turns gold?

whose hand in the water whose handkerchief and slow
    grief whose flip-flops covered with sand?
did anyone see footprints filled with child did someone
    reach and touch a warm shoulder turning?

horses plod along the bank raising dust and sweat they
    haul the invisible load and voices call
calling for the bride in her black dress beneath the
    poplars or walking away from the willows

raking through water fish and reeds raking for a body
    rolling it over and over until it's hooked
tines tearing through clothes and grasping time rolling
    forward into the past and rolling on

moon reaches into water and tempts us but does not reach
    deep enough voices growing away
I had a boy she says I had a son and for a moment that is
    all for a moment she lives with that

gone like the bell-ringer's wife

gone like the bell-ringer's wife like the voice in the garden
    gone like the good ships and fair winds
how long since you've tasted your shadow licking it where
    it lingers on the white stucco wall?
and how long gone the story of old days your mother told
    before bedtime the story of the drowned sailor?

the storm was rolling in and gods were weeping did we hear
    that sound the gods were leaving earth
did we hear the door close the blue door at the top of the
    steps did we hear our rude words to strangers?
we turned from them the wind riding through the orchard
    shaking drunken fruit to the ground

sometimes we thought we heard them talking faintly as if
    through a veil words at the root of us
sometimes we ran across paths that were still warm animal
    or god it was always hard to tell
and when the world went silent for a while we asked the
    band to strike up we learned not to whisper

everything sank beneath the sea the silver spears and
    buckles the basins and the banquetbowls
islands swamped one by one the islands disappeared
    leaving nothing but summer and flotsam behind
and people prayed with thick tongues they worshipped
    like cattle bawling in the noonday heat

did we see her lying beneath the wreckage of her dress
    on her elbows and arching her back?
always there was night at the stream's mouth and a way
    through night seed dropping into the rift
the bell tolled three times the rope uneasy as the
    bell-ringer dragged his feet toward the empty house

anna and rose

and the bleak tree the black tree standing in grass
    leafless in summer an arm rising from a grave
the calligraphy and notation of a pulse in god's terrain
    or something vanishing always vanishing

the bones of a horse legbone and ribcage a foal perhaps a
    small idea of a death cantering by
a small notion in a field an inland sea and the inhuman
    reach that holds so much human desire

so it goes with anna and rose with all those from before
    the ones who learned time very well
and no one to pass it on no one to sit on a stone and talk
    no one to remember you or the black tree

those who crossed this field the horse that stood in the
    shade and rubbed its hide against the bark
anna holding generations in her lap singing her childish
    songs before she put away her stuffed lamb

rose walking to her wedding her dress trailing behind her
    sisters laughing and unsnagging their skirts
sunday there was nothing all day but time and green stains
    and the breathless bride on the steps

alma

who was it who said who was it who called from the roof
   who was it who took off her flesh?

and when she moved into other worlds that one or another
   were they as voluptuous as this one?

her feet in sand as she walked down the beach her hands
   sticky with liquor did she recall anything?

had she called in the first place when she crawled out of
   the ruins had she called for anyone?

having seen flashes of galaxies and cosmic noise all that
   endlessness did she pluck out her eyes?

and then when everything came back to her body and
   everything the body knows who was it?

when lightning seared her eyes what was it came to her
   what was the other life she hadn't lived?

where the sea ran in and slid over her feet where was she
   among the sea dreams and the gulls?

someone's radio playing bad news and worse music how
   far off were all the gods who ever lived?

did she know her life was more than all those she loved
   did she know her life was less than her life?

anointed

etched shoulder blade and rib he's that thin and power
    lines across the sky
a shadow behind the drapes waiting for a son the boy
    tumbling from a drunken car

pouring wonder oil on his head she tries to massage
    away the lucifer
spinning wheels in diamond muck a light among the
    grinding gears

he is silent with spinning words nothing to get him out
    this night
and she has none no still words only a mother's song

white walls covered with graffiti covered with quotations
    on the walls of a mind
lacerations and low german jokes my god photos of ava
    joey and lollobrigida

everything the garden holds and one-legged hollyhocks
    leaning into the moon
the murmur of two or three languages among the raspberries
    and corn

she massages his brain praying the demons out and out
    and out
all in the name of the lord but her curiosity low-burning
    like a bunsen flame

the planet of a man spinning away into copse and ravine
    into the lapse of time
clocks and chimera the christers everywhere spinning
    toward absolution

all the fraud and wonder of cures the salvage of the
    utterly unsalvageable
the scent of it words and gestures the whole holy
    miscalculation

and for a moment he can't wish the smell away can't turn
    from the smoke
rising like a song *gute abend, gut' nacht* she sings

the sweet oil of love that penance that weight
gute abend and the waters of cutthroat love

lower fish street

who were you? there was a time a time when you were
    and I smelled you passing by that time and that time
moving toward lower fish street a river of sperm spittle
    on the water you passing every time all the time
shrugging on your white shirt your blazing shirt your thick
    fingers working at the small buttons by memory
and that was the last time you were and who were you?
    all of you escaping like invisible writing on the wall
the moon clear as a cold winter's night tipping over a
    wall a slice of silver filled with stones and birth
and gone when the door claps closed and then flies open
    what is it called what is the moment called?

and it happens all the time every day everything I
    remember grows to approximation and filament
the bulbs get shot out I hear them pop and I turn for a
    moment because I don't know what it is
I catch a worried face watching me then turn away and who
    turned away was it me or was it you?
who were you in my gaze? you and the weather and the
    sound of your feet crunching in the careless snow
but it's you who were with me almost like one man who
    fathered me for a while and then left for good and all
and nothing's good in endless vanish a loss incalculable
    intolerable and the rest of us at loose ends

and who you were was a scent almost a body a hint of
    something hooked like a call through the screen door
the coffin fell and broke open the old story of captivity
    and you released and flying from the tree
unraveling garments khaki work shirts a sunday fedora
    and the withered caul a million years old
christ how the christs are born again and again and seed
    spills and eggs drop and who it was you were
nothing no longer but an earthly stone sentiment and
    prodigious memory who can hold it in hand?
the river and the stream uncles casting their lines once
    more aunties spreading the table cloth again

let the sun shine a shadow across their graves

what was it how did it all come together this way of
belief or people the pampered boys the girls behind doors
what was this town the industry of it the wild bicycle paths
we flew along until it was time until it was time
the perfume of martyrdom never lost in the factory stench
the plumes of memory on the altar the blooms
of snow flowers the white blossoms in the cemetery
who could ever get through who could bury the dead
let the dead bury the dead someone said afraid of life
or maybe not that at all but let the dead stay dead
sent away with fire and let the sun
shine a shadow across their graves
let the winter arrive and leave let the rivers freeze
and what was it these people came from what
in the world was so bleak in the marrow
the bone fires of the final idea the *seelenangst*
long dead nothing remembered no child's play
no groan of love nothing growling in her ear
bodies naked and spread-eagled
let it all be forgotten judgment too
let a stranger's hands lay out my clothes

a greasy sax solo

skidding like a greasy sax solo sliding between heavenly
    and dirt rootless in the misery of world
almost a slug that ecstasy squirming on a grain of salt
    impaled on a want and wanting the want

and what comes after what comes after the solo what
    comes when the exhilaration pales into itself?
you lower your glass to the table lit with your
    extraordinary dreams you're coming down coming down

and there's a grace to it though you resist you want to stay
    crazy anything to keep your feet on fire
nerves exhausted you find a bench and looking around you
    bring out your comb waiting for someone

what do you do with the child tugging at your sleeve what
    do you do with that old man on the swing?
you want to comb god's hair but no one arrives and you're
    left restless pulling old strands from the teeth

your hands go cold in the moonlight hair drifting down the
    sidewalk and music dying in the distance
there's nothing much but the empty playground and a figure
    emerging from the club with a saxophone in its case

an empty dress hanging from the sky

she sings that she'll offer your hair to the saints you
    mustn't cry though you don't know what it means
she sings about blossoms she will throw into the fire and
    you keep splitting wood into kindling

she dances beneath an empty dress hanging from the sky
    her musicians playing bottles and spoons
she arches her naked back across the river where you have
    waited your life for a moment to cross

she holds your feet in her small hands in her eyes are the
    cities veils and deserts of the east
she brushes hair behind her ear fingers pausing at the lobe
    as she remembers her next words

she draws a map of her village to confuse you on your way
    a map of songs seeds and furrows
she shakes her head laughing leaving you with almost
    nothing but a splinter in your thumb

one foot on the platform

moonlight furrows across blue-black water arriving then
    glancing off your cadaverous face
when you move a moment later you're glowing seraphic
    or something strange and oddly beautiful

enamoured and beloved that human distress and the tales
    of flaw and miss and the short-circuit of romance
whoever wrote the book of love doo wop or dark mallory
    you come through it all with something intact

with one foot on the platform you look back this was your
    place in another station you'd never seen
the foreigner who has always come from another town
    another country you look for a waving hand

an old man you swing on a gate in july heat wondering
    where your balance went where the night went
waking some mornings with a cramp in your foot and a
    birthday party in the neighbour's yard

beside a wheelbarrow and an axe you pile the winter's
    wood in a lean-to november rain on your back
standing straight you gather your senses measuring hours
    once more as your father did in another time

juncos at the birdfeeder last exhalations from the garden
    nothing ever quite what it was or will be
the water of your first home has shifted shapes many times
    and once again it's waiting to fall as snow

koestler's window

it's what we're all born to koestler's window a spanish
    jail and the unredeemed math of death
a telephone ringing at the end of the hall with its lonely
    alphabet waiting to come together as a sentence
and history doesn't matter nor prophecy only the window
    with its flagrant insufferable possibilities

it is your shaking day call it that the day when all you
    ever knew is shaken into what you know
there is not a new thing you can name though the sun rises
    in the east and wouldn't you know it sinks in the west
your afternoon in the lawn chair among the montbretia has
    not done it but the sudden shiver at dusk maybe

the way you wake inside the hours of daylight the way you
    rise from that awful ungodly slumber
half-awake hanging onto the threads of a dream of home
    street waking from the perfect garden
or waking back into the deepest sleep of rivers and all
    you've forgotten carried in that current

the rum's run out the sun setting on brentwood bay and
    all the buses are leaving butchart gardens
there's no relief no getting past it the bicycle gets you
    nowhere and tourists pin their hopes on you
orthodox women with their lopsided wigs won't shake
    your hand and nuns won't bear your child

the window is open staring in at your rumpled sheets and
    gazing out at the stain of mountains
the telephone dangles black and stiff from the wall a
    garbled voice ranting amongst the dying footfalls
beneath your sill a dog circles the soil of its sleep
    settling with a sigh among the closed red tulips

o'keeffe bones

a place where you never heard thunder not thunder not the
    sound that reaches into you for a moment and leaves
leaving nothing behind to hold you nothing to terrify
    leaving nothing but the rubble of a fallen city
it's a place you can't return to there is too much going on
    the only church you love to enter is the empty one
sitting at the back always near the door and no one in
    sight you listen for the sound that was left behind

awake in the pew rafters and hymns and stained glass the
    stations of the cross around all that want
and you sully the emptiness with your body the smell of
    worry of world the smell of your birth
alive you sit there in your memory and memory before
    that knowing everything always leaves
you sit there and don't belong to what you see or know
    you belong to nothing but what you hear

and what you hear is what you heard or what you think
    you heard echo fade and doppler effect
what you don't hear anymore is the word any word you
    don't hear solace and there is no astonishment
what you hear is the wind in march or perhaps july or
    that exhalation you think you hear at night
human ruin the serenity of the building fallen what is
    there is the sun on o'keeffe bones beside a white wall

cross-wired

cross-wired between the chicken coop's dust and cackle
    and the hellish heat of the lord's back rooms
doubled in the hall mirror on sunday morning drawn and
    quartered with the sweetest love in the world
something cross-wise in the song raised to the roof all
    dirge and purged of anything you might want to sing
the raw dialect of the barn a pail of milk knocked over
    and grandfather beating the cow with a board

well there's no history anymore is there that's all done
    with no history no home to ever return to
nothing here now that was there then nothing but some
    memory of memory nostalgia has its moments
all the stories criss-crossed you can't tell them apart can't
    tell truth from truth good god what are you saying?
you're going blind from staring at the light soon you'll be
    singing like those blind russian singers on back roads

where does this anger come from this arrhythmia you
    can't regulate just like that these spasms of breath
and the pang you don't want to recognize is the pain
    that's not possible to quarantine from love
those days in the desert indulging your ascetic
    disappearance trying to name what doesn't need a name
or trying to lose your name like an immigrant who believes
    things can begin again as if they've ever begun

good god what are you saying? someone's in the coop with
    an axe and you don't want to know the rest
everyone's on best behavior at a funeral that's where you
    write the parts for all the others but you
and you where on earth are you? the wind whipping up a
    dust devil is as close to spirit as you get
yeah nothing wrong with blind and ill-shod on a dirt road
    whistling your way into another tune

one summer night at la bodega

your life changes at la bodega one summer night that
    begins with the lassitude of feeling unloved
several litres of sangria and stolen tears of nostalgia
    lead eventually to sobriety in the back of a taxi
and glancing through the rear window you see two
    women one who has been your lover waving goodbye
this is a woman who once told you the pain you felt had
    already moved on to another fool
those weren't her precise words but it's what you needed
    to hear it's what she gave to you freely
you wonder how a lover becomes a friend without love
    going lost and you turn to the rear view mirror
later you stand on the railing of your balcony as if
    sailing toward the open door of your last day
but you never buy the calendar with a date circled in red
    this is another thing you don't need to own
but you know at la bodega what the cabbie sees in your
    face you know that fidelity is wild

our lady of guadalupe

sliding into a pew in the empty church up to no good no
   belief nothing you can write down anyway
gazing at the stations of the cross and drawing a blank
   listening to the emptiness and the poverty in you

you're sitting in a place your people left long ago as if
   you might encounter something from before
tired of thought and throne wanting a moment of surprise
   any ritual the body can undermine

before before vigilance and the martyr's memory before
   that tale of the hammer and the cross
before the inside duel and the immersion of heaven the
   human hand denied before that before suicide

but what of this place a solace of release the cribbed notes
   and narratives what fears and surrenders?
is there something that slipped away something startling
   and true something you can smell or hear?

is there a footprint on the threshold a faint print you
   bend to see closely and perhaps the smell of a foot?
you touch it with your fingers but there's no warmth it's
   a stone that holds neither scent nor memory

so you listen for echo the distant noises of traffic entering
   and fading as a door opens and closes and opens
you listen for a godless uncertainty and a million years
   of fatigue you listen for the unexpected word

and she says why speak of it

oh so for you to reach for the lie again how you love
the lie of god and can't help yourself and she says why
speak of it and you glow through your eyes knowing what
she knows but unable to shutter your mind and mouth of
all that praise of words and ecstasy all that gift of gab
and god and you may as well admit that it's earth that
voluptuous taste that raspberry and the rough flesh of
your fingers sliding along silk it makes you shiver it's
earth and perfume that's sap on your tongue it's that it's
all of that and the more some shattered soul of you
glimpses and needs the more the lie of love the longing
on the skin of words and she asks why speak of it?

watering their graves with your blood

littered with animals the sky alive with the eyes of a bull
    starry antlers and the cattle of magdalena
a horse galloping you can see the way it moves across the
    uneven surface and the contours of mind
the cave your cave striations and the pigment of mind
    some mind that you juggle for a moment
everything was there in the world's brain men grunting
    and uttering in the tallow light of birth
and not birth but another day of thirst and work and longing
    and yes it was another day of birth

you pause you stop agog gawking like an idiot you have
    not become human you have not become
gelded and spayed there is a fungus in the cave if only you
    could lower yourself into the rosy sky
the sea does not look like wine but it did and when it did it
    held all of your undelivered body
and what have you got now a bowl of oranges on the table
    a tape measure and a pamphlet on health
for christ's sake peel that orange its scent on your fingers
    and let yourself go into the hallucination

who painted the dream you could never place what killer's
    hands drew the genetics of you
and before you before the water opened before the world
    took hold and before anyone thought to think?
you visit the cemetery all your grandparents that was
    yesterday their deaths have not yet come alive
watering their graves with your blood the blossoming
    children and the ancient dead in your brain
who breathed in the smoke of caves the colour the paint
    they made who never dreamed you

a long day's gaze into delirium

so many cadavers gone to ground along river banks in
    caves and at the edges of cliffs and clearings
a bee at the lip of a lily for a thousand years and you
    watching your garden as if it's the first

whose arms those cadavers of yours the longing for them
    for the particulars of unnamed days
what they smelled the rank river or fish scales on their
    hands and wood-fire smoke in their hair

the brain of the map its stones and scorched trees earth
    lit from inside the sun barely on fire
a birth canal death rattle is the music feet shuffling in
    the dust of a long day's gaze into delirium

horizon takes you down from your dancing on the roof
    horses skittering across your waking dream
stray birds and stars on the screen of your eyelids they're
    fast light flashing in the thunder of the cave

a bee at the lip of the birth canal the smell of the river
    on their hands and skittish horses gone to ground
the sun on fire like delirium like the brain of the map
    scorched from inside feet shuffling inside the thunder

perfectly alive at the edge of light

who bent that relentless note the note that tore at your
    sleeve whose finger bent that note?
and that note bending around you sitting there drinking
    at a sloppy table in the railway club
taut as a string you bending into the sexual drunken night
    cutting your ties with a wintry blade
and there's nothing new here the blade has old blood on it
    your own the grease that slid you by
that note bending through the open window to the traffic
    the slick traffic and its human refuse
and your hand is shaking as it always has your eyes blue
    coals and you alive at the edge of light
at least that's your take as the note bends around the
    room your fever heading toward zero
and you can refuse nothing not the wind nor the ice of it
    you can't refuse the cough of winter

room 205

living above the paragon gazing at the sandstone shine
    of st. mary's in late light
bags of rain hanging over the steeple and caught in some
    contradiction of time

somewhere in this city you made a voice somewhere in the
    blinding snow
and that open window across the street with the white
    curtains billowing out

or casting your thin wallet to the fishes off the old
    midtown bridge
a poppy in your lapel and a frayed panama stained with
    sweat

that ancient hand rising from the assiniboine to catch
    your loot
and on the river bank a bride and groom posing for
    photographs

you're watching the dirty water of your bath swirl down
    the drain
some of you flowing beneath the history of this city and
    the weather

sand blowing down the streets and you're begging for what
    you need
they will take your shoes they will kill until you've earned
    your anxiety

there never was a code to break but futility is a life like
    life
you were not shot by a uniform you were not given over
    to heaven

ohhh and just now old man jimmy next door pulls a false
    alarm
he's thinking way back and trying to live dangerously one
    more time

one man's world disappears every day his virtue always
    turns him in
but there are a few who pause to take photographs that
    kind of light and frame

and there is only what? your lover and your children names
    at the end of a letter
as usual you singing out of tune that famous song of
    extinction that anonymity

nonno facing the sun

earth heats up in april the blue sun burning through a
    haze of distance and a few careless clouds
a boy's birthday party in his back yard balloons dogs and
    burgers and the eternity of mom and dad
across the fence his disease at bay and his eyes closed
    nonno sits in a lawnchair against a worn brick wall
light dazzling his white hair his frail voice swallowing
    he could be rewinding to the time of bicycles
his legs pumping for roma and home through a landscape
    of sun and artillery and gods in the rubble
nonno in this last spring his lean legs akimbo before him
    and the garden spade leaning against the wall
his hands folded on his lap nonno facing the sun a daughter
    in the grave another watching from the window
nonno reaches blindly for a hoe to hold across his knees
    the garden gone to grass and the shed filled with eyes

nothing comes to you that won't come later

lying flat-out on a stone-cold tile floor the spanish sun
    through the window burns you away
turning and flexing to ease your northern spine you twist
    until there's nothing left but getting up
you rise with dust and hair on your back trying to remember
    the day and time of your return flight
and nothing comes to you because of mojácar and valparaíso
    nothing comes to you that won't come later

and what came before from the north the poplar and willow
    it must have been an earthly birth
some kind of northern story you have to live out for the
    sins and tribulations driving you through
snorting you wish the sins were bigger worth something
    more than guilt who wants to die stupid?
but the blood is hot says mellissa and you hope maybe it
    holds something phoenician or tartar

what comes from the scarlet saint old woman who loved
    you before you were born who loved the seed
but you slept through that or too busy crawling through
    the door you scraped your knee on the sill
my god how many times are you going to do that before you
    learn this shit goes on and on
and the old woman gave you the eye it's all you have to
    know and what you will know

moriarty said there is no terminus only departure and
    you want to believe the blessed man for what he was
but was that belief or fumbling for the rosary in his irish
    pocket just a little chagrin in his laughter?
nimble hobgoblin dancing through the canon there
    would always be a last day of measure ahead
take it all apart baby and put it together again that's all
    take it all apart and put it together again

there are days you stare at the mule all day and days you
    remember women you hoped would want you
but that's ass backwards better stick with the mule get
    something done before the sky goes red
that's the ploughman in you one eye on the furrow the
    other on heaven you never know what falls down
and you wonder about the weather in white mojácar on
    a hill or that worried town on the prairies

mongolian radio ray price fiddles hank locklin and spruce tree sighs

the one who washed another man's feet who sat at table
  with a whore
can't think him in a country of greed and leering with its
  fear of all the other
the great enterprise of rendering man and woman into
  the holy machine
who eats the christ feeding off misery and the angry
  tongue?

such a death this one of the hammer this ghost of god
  hammering at our ears
where it comes from is anywhere but from inside the
  grave of the mother's womb
love death when it's yours but turn from the one the
  christers nail to the sky
we all ravage our own killing the wild child stifling
  . that sudden inhalation

listen to the sound of everything honest every note and
  word every call
a dove on the wire the mule braying against the sun a
  tenderness in the telephone
the wind across a yellow field a meister eckhart wind
  the river's still wind
listening to mongolian radio ray price fiddles hank
  locklin and spruce tree sighs

never heard such a sound a praise never heard such a
    jackfish wind
rippling across the water's skin raising every hook and
    line ever thrown
well listen there is a song gone to ground a fibre between
    root and node
woven through the great desire of the urgent world

a man dipping his foot in the creek a woman washing
    her long black hair
there's not much else but the poems and sermons some
    of us can't hold back
always those strangers standing awkward in a black and
    white photograph
and always the graveyards with their stones carved *safe*
    in the arms

goya's room

where he sat beneath a dark window a dog caught in its
    festering life
beyond baying or the moon or anything like that just
    gazing at the brazen night and
a long year of deaths and empty rooms and mouths open
    with sentences
things said he remembers vaguely the drift or perhaps
    a precise phrase

with no word that works only that it is unsaid only that
    it happens only that things
disappear and for him that is forever legs slipping
    deeper in muck

he has not wasted enough time he thinks he has not
    listened to enough music
not taken in enough winter light or strings of pearls he
    has not stopped counting the days

thinking he has done too much of death's work that
    usefulness to the machine
shifting gears or pumping the brakes one year wrapping
    windows to be installed
in heaven they said there was not even the dignity of
    dying but a small spittle of greed

on thursday night he dreams of water the splash of a
    kingfisher his lover's eyes
how they suddenly glisten with a quicksilver of
    tenderness
dreaming on the weekend of a silken gown the red of no
    flowers
but the red of a certain blood perhaps

understanding he has not done enough of death's work
    that uselessness
that drenched black suit he can't take off his fingers
    locked in the gloves
crossed on his chest that delight of undoing what he has
    not done doing nothing
on his back the bartender staring up at the lit jewels of
    bottles behind him
remembering every brilliant face and bracelet every
    carpenter with a black thumb
and every story-teller with a stutter that he watered

so it goes in his room with shutters battened against the
    smell of damp
earthy night the heat of fire in the river sliding through
    him and
the old dancer with serpent arms with a famous story on
    her hips
and the desire of her flaring nostrils he applauds what
    he saw
in the eye of the stage and what he can't hold

he throws himself at walls scorched walls one winter
    night throwing himself
into the depth of a man only a man one mind's man and the
    fire guttering out

he works there in the room blowing on the embers and
    arranging himself into disarray

blue-eyed son of a brown-eyed son

a blue-eyed son of a brown-eyed son of a runaway horizon
love and perish at the window a ruthless tango of loneliness
and the egyptian descends into the delta's flood

a dickinsonian night with brown fog beneath street lamps
a lanky gatekeeper sweeping leaves off sunken graves
and the slow exhalation moves through the grass

fire he cried from the tree moonlight wearing him down
the blind man on his knees in the field waiting for snow
and the angel lurches into the grazing herd

on a bone pile in the ditch a sapling through a socket
crushed grass where the wheel has rolled
and the reed bends beneath the bird

not a clock but the shovel wakes the drowsy man
staring like giacometti down the dark hallway
and lights flicker with the storm

he remembers a crucified snake he sings of a dog
a child's urchin ways blessed a mischief in a tree
and he hangs on like rain

lucifer

raise your arms for whatever saint or slain sinner you
    surrender to in a moment of bondage
selah selah and salaam all the heat of desert and the
    water's clear moment the fathers in their graves

montbretia in the garden a dozen scarlet butterflies
    perched on a stem rising above the green blades
you're waiting for them to leave earth like the blackbird's
    red patch fluttering on a reed you wait
lucifer lit by the afternoon sun lucifer on fire the fire of
    his god the fire of refusal and pride
lift your hat to your death you are dying today and you
    will be dying for a long time lift your hat

they are leaving earth the lurid butterflies are always
    leaving shining in this simmering bordello
you haven't known that until this garden on this day well
    you haven't known anything until now
the calls to salvation the troubled tread of steel-toed
    boots all of it disappears like a magic trick
and it is a trick everything is a trick of your life a trick
    of the dead all the love left behind

a pentecostal shout such a dark spirit and someone turning
    slowly in the garden raising praise
is that lorca clapping hands is that a broken rifle is that
    the dirt road that never stops traveling?

ecstatic to arrive

sky divers are all experts of the cold sky kiss they are
    lonely astronauts far from the water of doubt
their chutes trailing above them divers with their narrow
    hunter eyes plummet toward the endless flocks
that moment that verge and vertigo the rank stench of
    vegetation and animal rising with a sigh
that enters them as they fall and them entering bird after
    bird earth's red wings at their shoulders
smoldering inside their wings and glowing dim as embers
    all memory splintering and being born
sky divers have forgotten what they've left but they are
    ecstatic to arrive in the heat of the hours

loose in the house of fundamentalism

you go dancing around your room banging off red walls
     pictures swinging wildly on their hooks
shivers down your backbone tailfeathers ruffling and you
     playing piano with a ball peen hammer

words and doors unhinged as night blooms in the brain's
     soil flowering like the watered grave
you're flagrant and lost sniffing for primal heat kicking
     your way through the room's furniture

nighthawk or crow this is the word loose in the house of
     fundamentalism wings beating against glass
cries of blue fire anger's call for vengeance rocking on
     your toes knocking the clock from the wall

a quiver in your bones old as old but who's counting bog
     piltdown man and lucy in the sky
bestial and defrocked some god undone with one blue eye
     lazy and the other dark and crazy

you skid scuffing linoleum all feathers and mischief
     careless damage along the million mile wall
bitching at some yellow-eyed parrot *not enough* nothing
     memorized just holy ghost and a slippery foot

wella wella sings the crow *bird is the word* hopping from
     leg to leg a cockeyed killer and awry
wella wella next flight out of here heading anywhere and
     anything goes and always it does

collecting bottles

what did you say in your bio what was the story after
    that and who did you mention in passing?

biking along town line road what were you hearing
    what invisible motion swayed the tall grasses?

who gathered sun and clouds who gathered the bicycle
    wheels and rolled all toward the horizon?

where are the histories of those who live in dreams those
    walking toward graves no one will visit?

stopping on the shoulder the two of you straddling your
    bikes did you know this was everything?

how were you built in this place for this light your bones
    grown from this soil and from these people?

when you had nothing in mind pedaling through the
    overlap of memory did you come to yourself?

cashing in your bottles for a pepsi at betty's grocery you
    leaned into your shadow on the white stucco wall

poem for jonah

I will carry you through the streets of madrid or lisboa
I will carry you through the end of my time toward the
    fullness of yours

whatever else I've carried my shoulders are the shoulders
    of those before me
shoulders that carried shovels and shawls shoulders
    carrying the black and heavy book

and these shoulders hold the light of a helpless town skin
    burned and burning
holding the words and music of an era of glory and
    deception and always work

I will carry you as I carried your mother as she carries
    you and you will carry
your son or daughter and one day you will carry me

and the questions   have I arrived?
and if I have not arrived how do I go?

ACKNOWLEDGEMENTS

Some of these poems were published in *Malahat Review,
The Winnipeg Review, Dream Catcher 23, Prairie Fire, CVII,
Rhubarb, and subTerrain.*

Many thanks to the Fundácion Valparaíso in Spain for the
opportunity to work there in 2010. And thank-you to the
BC Arts Council for financial assistance.

Remembering P. K. Page for her generosity and elegance
of spirit, and for the many wonderful conversations.

Richard Hildebrand and Margie Gillis for on-going
inspiration.

Marijke Friesen for her work on the cover, and Eve Joseph
for pretty much everything.